piano • vocal • guitar

the best of

BARRY MANILOW

ISBN 0-7935-3423-2

HAL•LEONARD™
CORPORATION
7777 W. BLUEMOUND RD. P.O. BOX 13819 MILWAUKEE, WI 53213

Dear Friends,

Here's a new collection of some of my favorite songs. I'm very proud to have been associated with these tunes and hope you have a good time with them.

"Who Needs To Dream" has never before appeared in print. The song comes from our movie "Copacabana" and got me my first screen kiss. Hope you get lucky with it too!

Enjoy!

Barry

piano • vocal • guitar

the best of
BARRY MANILOW

ALL THE TIME

Words and Music by BARRY MANILOW
and MARTY PANZER

All the time I thought there's on - ly me,
All the time I thought that I was wrong

cra - zy in a way that no - one else could be.
want - ing to be me, but need - ing to be - long.

I would have giv - en ev - 'ry - thing I own if
If I had just be - lieved in all I had, if

CAN'T SMILE WITHOUT YOU

Words and Music by CHRIS ARNOLD,
DAVID MARTIN and GEOFF MORROW

14

15

COULD IT BE MAGIC

Words and Music by ADRIENNE ANDERSON
and BARRY MANILOW

Ba-by I want_ you.

tacet

D. S.al Coda %

21

COPACABANA
(AT THE COPA)

Words by BRUCE SUSSMAN and JACK FELDMAN
Music by BARRY MANILOW

23

24

DAYBREAK

Words by ADRIENNE ANDERSON
Music by BARRY MANILOW

EVEN NOW

Words by MARTY PANZER
Music by BARRY MANILOW

I WRITE THE SONGS

Words and Music by
BRUCE JOHNSTON

I MADE IT THROUGH THE RAIN

Words and Music by BARRY MANILOW, JACK FELDMAN,
BRUCE SUSSMAN, DREY SHEPPERD and GERARD KENNY

Warm Ballad

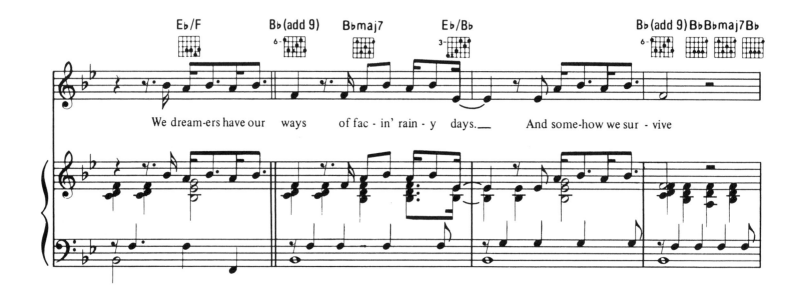

We dream-ers have our ways of fac-in' rain-y days.__ And some-how we sur-vive

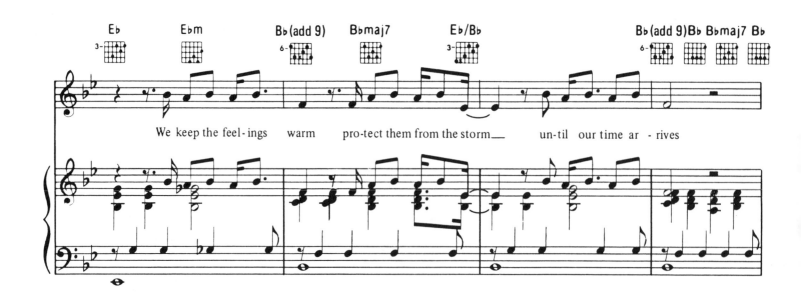

We keep the feel-ings warm pro-tect them from the storm__ un-til our time ar-rives

I Made It Through The Rain____ I kept my world pro-tec-ted I Made It Through_The Rain__ I

kept my point of view I Made It Through__ The Rain____ And found my-self re-spec-ted by the

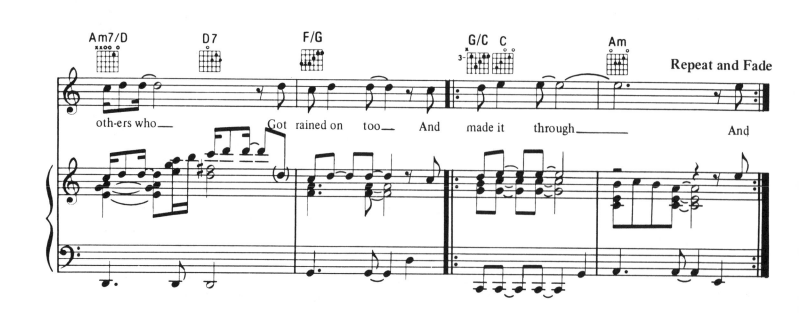

oth-ers who___ Got rained on too__ And made it through_____ And

Repeat and Fade

IF I SHOULD LOVE AGAIN

Words and Music by
BARRY MANILOW

46

47

IT'S A MIRACLE

Words by BARRY MANILOW and MARTY PANZER
Music by BARRY MANILOW

IF YOU WERE HERE WITH ME TONIGHT

Music by ERIC BORENSTEIN and BARRY MANILOW
Lyric by ERIC BORENSTEIN and LISA SENNETT THOMAS

63

LOOKS LIKE WE MADE IT

Words by WILL JENNINGS
Music by RICHARD KERR

MANDY

Words and Music by SCOTT ENGLISH
and RICHARD KERR

MEMORY

Lyrics by TREVOR NUNN and T.S. ELIOT
Music by ANDREW LLOYD WEBBER

NEW YORK CITY RHYTHM

Words and Music by BARRY MANILOW
and MARTY PANZER

THE OLD SONGS

Words and Music by DAVID POMERANZ
and BUDDY KAYE

Can-dles burn-ing, glass-es are chilled,_and soon ___ she'll be by.___

Hope and pray_ she'll say___ that she's will - ing to give us an-oth-er try. And

make her want to stay.____

ONE VOICE

Words and Music by
BARRY MANILOW

Slowly, with much feeling

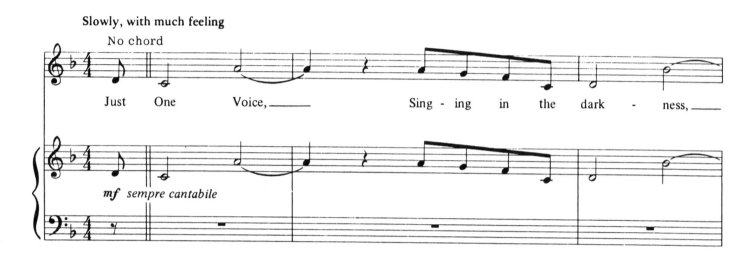

Just One Voice, _____ Sing - ing in the dark - ness, _____

_____ All it takes is One Voice, _____ Sing - ing so they

hear what's on your mind, And when you look a - round you'll find There's more than

94

SHIPS

Words and Music by
IAN HUNTER

PARADISE CAFE

Words by BRUCE SUSSMAN and JACK FELDMAN
Music by BARRY MANILOW

SOME KIND OF FRIEND

Words by ADRIENNE ANDERSON
Music by BARRY MANILOW

103

107

fan - ta - sy___ that___ you found___

Some kind, Some___ kind of friend . . . Some kind . . .

SOMEWHERE IN THE NIGHT

Words by WILL JENNINGS
Music by RICHARD KERR

THIS ONE'S FOR YOU

Words by MARTY PANZER
Music by BARRY MANILOW

TRYIN' TO GET THE FEELING AGAIN

Words and Music by
DAVID POMERANZ

122

WEEKEND IN NEW ENGLAND

Words and Music by
RANDY EDELMAN

126

WHEN OCTOBER GOES

Words by JOHNNY MERCER
Music by BARRY MANILOW

130

WHO NEEDS TO DREAM

Words by BRUCE SUSSMAN and JACK FELDMAN
Music by BARRY MANILOW and ARTIE BUTLER

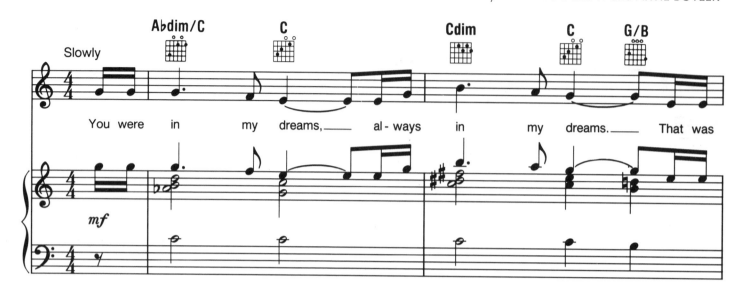

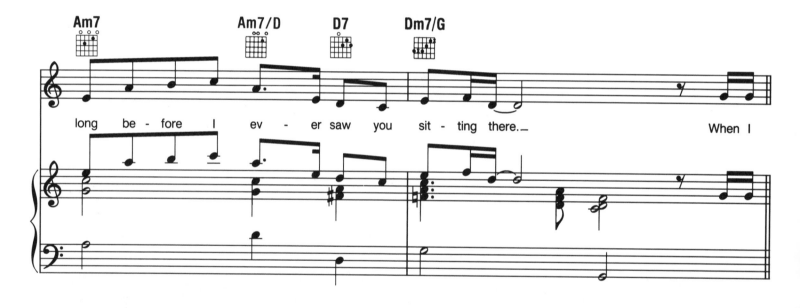

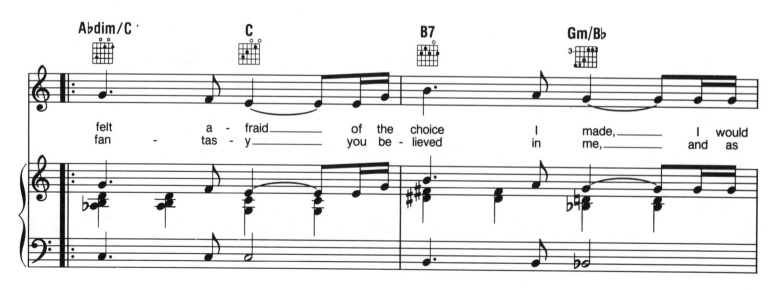

Am7/D
D7
1 G(add 9)
dream? You're my dream come true.
C(add9)
2 G(add 9)
Dm7/G
In my true.
C
Fm6/C
C(add9)
F/C
Now you are my dream. You are my
C
G/B
G/A
Am7
Am7/G
Fmaj7
G/F
on - ly dream.
I'll hold you in my heart for -